PER ARDUA PRO PATRIA

To Pam.
with sincere best wishes
Den Wiltshire
30/01/04

Pax vobiscum

Published in 2000 by
WOODFIELD PUBLISHING
Bognor Regis, West Sussex PO21 5EL, UK.

© Dennis Wiltshire, 2000

ISBN 0 873203 50 0

Per Ardua
Pro Patria

*Autobiographical
observations of a
World War II Airman*

DENNIS WILTSHIRE

Woodfield *Publishing*
BOGNOR REGIS · WEST SUSSEX · ENGLAND

Contents

I wish to dedicate this book to the following people:

Firstly, to my late dear wife, Josephine, with whom I spent over fifty of the most happy years;

Next to my son, Michael, and his wife, Christine, who, despite their busy lives, remained faithful to us and to me especially after the loss of my dear wife;

To my grandsons, Stephen and David, both of whom have not at any time forgotten their grandparents and have excelled themselves in the academic and professional world.

Finally , but by no means least, to my dear and closest friend, Roma, who, with my own family, brought me back to a normal life, after the depressive state into which I fell after the death of my dear wife.

"Semper Fidelis".

Introduction

The contents of this portfolio are a compilation of events in my life. Perhaps inconsequential to many readers, even uninteresting to some, but each individual incident has left a strong influence on my journey through life.

I trust the contents will prove of some interest to all who read them.

Dennis A.Wiltshire
FRAS. FAIAA. ARAeS. FIMgt. HON R.A. (BRISTOL)

ACKNOWLEDGEMENTS

I am indebted to many people for their assistance in enabling me to bring this manuscript to fruition:-

The Royal Air Force Records Department.

Southmead Hospital Trust.

U.S.A. National Aeronautics & Space Administration

and many friends and colleagues.

My most sincere thanks go to my dear daughter-in-law, who has given me support and many hours of her valuable time to produce this final transcript.

Dennis 'Lofty' Wiltshire, in RAFVR uniform, 1940.

PER ARDUA PRO PATRIA

About the Author

Educated in Clifton in Bristol, Dennis Wiltshire went on to study automobile engineering at the Society of Merchant Venturers Technical College. In 1939 he relinquished both his studies and apprenticeship to join the RAFVR. Here he acquired further engineering skills, being posted to both No.2 and No.10 Schools of Technical Training, eventually becoming a Junior N.C.O. Fitter 11E (Aero-Engine Fitter)

After a short stint of duty with Fighter Command during the Battle of Britain, he was posted overseas to Canada, where he served for two years at No.36 Service Flying Training School, working and flying with Airspeed Oxford aircraft as part of the Commonwealth Air Training Plan.

On his return to the U.K. in 1943, he remustered and trained as a Flight Engineer. He served with both 82 and 90 Squadrons as Flight Engineer on Lancaster Bomber Aircraft, but on his final mission suffered a complete mental and physical breakdown. He was hospitalized at an RAF hospital in Derbyshire until his medical discharge from the RAF in mid 1944.

Despite his first setback in 1944 and the five years of hospitalisation and frustration that followed, he fought back to regain a position in the field of aerospace technology, when in 1952 he joined the technical staff of Rolls-Royce Ltd. With a team of other technicians and engineers, he prepared and wrote overhaul and maintenance manuals for world famous aero-engines such as the Bristol Proteus, Viper and Olympus engines.

During his final years at Rolls-Royce he became involved in the Research and Development of the Pegasus Engine, the power-plant installed in the now famous Hawker Harrier V.T.O.L. (jump-jet) aircraft.

Apart from the rigours of the critical work involved in the preparation of pilots and ground staff instruction manuals for this particular aircraft, Dennis was now also working in close liaison with NASA on the Apollo Programme at Langley Research Station and Ames Research Centre in USA.

For his efforts in the field of technical authorship, aerospace technology and space medicine, the "American Institute of Aeronautics and Astronautics" awarded him an Associate Fellowship with the Institute, an award also held by several Astronauts and back-up crews. In England his work was rewarded by the award of Fellowships in the British Interplanetary Society, Institute of Scientific and Technical Communicators, and the Institute of Management Specialists.

During the Apollo Programme Mr Wiltshire devoted a considerable amount of time to Space Technology "Spin-Off Benefits", and his work and reports were followed up by such establishments as The British Ship Research Association, The International Council of Science Teaching, Massey Ferguson (Australia) Ltd., The University of Dayton Ohio, The United Nations and many other authoritative organisations.

After a further long illness and hospitalization in 1972, at the suggestion of hospital consultants, he retired from active life and together with his wife, who died in 1994, devoted his life to charitable institutions including the Women's Royal Voluntary Service, the Royal Air Forces Association, the Soldiers', Sailors' and Airmen's Families Association, and the League of Hospital and Community Friends.

CHAPTER 1

A Concise History of RAF Cosford

The Royal Air Force Station at RAF Cosford was opened in 1938 as part of the Government's prewar expansion policy for armed services. It was primarily to be a technical training school but. although this has always been its major role, Cosford also became the home of an important RAF Hospital and over the years has had a number of other maintenance and training tasks.

From 1939 to 1942 Cosford was one of three Officer Training Schools for ground branch officers. Between 1942 and 1943 the three Officer Training Schools were amalgamated at Cosford as the Officer Cadet Training Unit. This unit was transferred to Spitalgate in 1948 and after moves is now at Cranwell.

The RAF School of Catering was at Cosford from 1954 to 1958 when it moved to Hereford.

The second unit to be set up at Cosford was No.9 Maintenance Unit (9MU), which was to be opened as an Aircraft Storage Unit in 1939. The task of this unit was to store, assemble , repair and maintain all types of aircraft from Tiger Moths to Vickers Wellington bombers. It would then ferry required aircraft to the appropriate operational unit. The main types of aircraft handled by 9MU were Spitfire, Mosquito, Beaufighter and Wellingtons. However in July 1942 the unit went into full time glider production of the Airspeed Horsa. The first Horsa glider was produced on the 30th July 1942 and by November had assembled fifty plus. Cosford was only one of two units to undertake such production, the other unit being at Brize Norton in Oxfordshire. As a result many of the gliders assembled here were to take part in the invasion of Europe and also Operation Market Garden (the allied airborne assaults at Arnhem and Nijmegan, Holland).

Throughout the war period many enemy attacks were made in the Birmingham/Wolverhampton area and as a result Vickers/ Supermarine moved a Spitfire production unit to Cosford. The Spitfire became one of the few aircraft to pass through Cosford to have been both produced and assembled here.

Cosford itself only suffered one enemy air raid throughout the war period. This took place on Tuesday 11th March, 1941 when the Luftwaffe launched a major attack on Birmingham (to the extent that over a two hour period more than 76 raids took place). At one point 135 Heinkel 111 and Junkers 88 aircraft targeted north-west Birmingham but were hampered by cloud, and as a result few were able to bomb visually. The Birmingham Anti-Aircraft guns fired nearly 7000 rounds of ammunition but with little success. Some of these aircraft strayed off course and suddenly appeared over Cosford. Incendiary bombs landed on the flying ground but were quickly extinguished by unit personnel as the raid continued. Two high explosive bombs narrowly missed a hangar but caused considerable damage to its end wall. Further HE bombs exploded in open countryside but succeeded in damaging access roads to dispersed aircraft. After the raid it was discovered that only two Lysander aircraft, located in the hangar, had been damaged and no injuries to personnel had been sustained.

When 9MU disbanded in 1956 it was replaced by No 236 Maintenance Unit who specialised in mechanical transport.

An RAF Hospital opened at Cosford in 1940 equipped with 503 beds. In 1941 a Burns Centre was established and the available beds increased to 612. Throughout the course of the war some 42,000 patients were admitted. The general decrease in the number of Servicemen in the West Midlands led to plans to close the hospital in 1975. This was forestalled by the request of the National Health Service and the hospital remained open until the end of 1977 for the benefit of the local civilian population. Cosford Hospital provided an excellent service and will undoubtedly be remembered gratefully by the many thousands of service and civilian patients who received treatment there over a period of 37 years.

NO 2 SCHOOL OF TECHNICAL TRAINING

The main unit at Cosford is, and always has been, No 2 School of Technical Training. In the summer of 1939 two apprentice training wings were in operation and some courses were also run for adults. With the outbreak of war, apprentice training had to give way for intensive training of adults. Some 70,000 engine and airframe mechanics and armourers attended war-time courses to enable them to convert to 'fitter' standard.

For some time after the war, training of airframe and engine mechanics continued. Gradually Cosford became orientated to its peacetime role of youth training, which was formally reintroduced in May 1950 with the arrival of Boy Entrants. By 1953, at the height of the scheme, there were 2,500 boys undergoing 18 month training courses. Educational and technical training naturally took up much of their time but character training played a very important part in the curriculum. Many boys participated in activities appropriate to the Duke of Edinburgh's Award Scheme.

When the trade structure of the Royal Air Force was substantially altered in 1964, a new approach to youth training was required. This meant the end of the Boy Entrant Scheme in July 1965. At Cosford the new scheme provided for Craft Apprentices, who took a one year course as Electronic Fitters. Technician apprentices undertook a three year course as Electronic Technicians (Air).

In the early 1970s the trend away from apprentice training resulted in the ending of the one and two year apprenticeships. The three year technician apprenticeships were phased out in March 1976 but were replaced by two new three year apprenticeships for the dual skilled trades of Electronic Engineering Technician (Air Communications and Air Radar) and Electronic Engineering Technician (Flight Systems).

The craft apprentice "fitters" (now renamed "technicians") were in all cases replaced by adult recruits, usually referred to as "Direct Entrants", who underwent the same trade training in a somewhat shorter time.

In May 1979 the armourers returned to Cosford, when Weapons Squadron was established to provide trade training for weapons technicians.

In 1989 an Aircraft Engineering Trades Review resulted in significant changes to the trade boundaries, methods of entry and training of Trade Groups 1 and 2. From 1 April 1991, a selective, single gate method of entry was introduced, with the replacement of Apprentices and Direct Entrants by common Basic Training. All recruits who possess 4 GCSE passes at grade C or above, including Mathematics and Physics, enter into a "Technician" stream. Recruits with lesser qualifications enter into a "Mechanic" stream. Common Basic Training is followed by 1 to 2 years productive service for the "Technician" stream entrants before they enter Technician Further Training. "Mechanic" stream entrants displaying outstanding technician potential during Basic Training may be offered transfer to the "Technician" stream. Those who remain in the "Mechanic" stream during productive service, may also be selected for Further Training on the basis on their performance and service requirements.

Many technicians come back to Cosford yet again for advanced "Pre-employment" courses on new avionic equipments or specialist weapons equipments. Overseas students, both airmen and officers, are also trained at Cosford.

JOINT SERVICES SCHOOL OF PHOTOGRAPHY (JSOP)

The RAF School of Photogaphy moved from Wellesbourne Mountford to Cosford in September 1963 and became a tri-Service School in April 1972. The Joint School of Photography is staffed with photographic training from all three Services and is staffed by officers, NCOs and junior ranks from the Navy, Army and RAF. The School is housed in a modern purpose-designed building which is one of the largest schools of photography in Europe. The major task is to train the tradesmen involved in processing of air reconnaissance and survey photography, and the servicing of air cameras installed in reconnaissance aircraft.

The School also trains the ground photographers for the Navy, Army and RAF, as well as running a variety of postgraduate or pre-employment courses, covering such areas as hydrographic survey, colour printing and photographic equipment servicing.

RAF SCHOOL OF PHYSICAL TRAINING

The RAF School of Physical Training celebrated its 60th anniversary on 1 April 1978. The School was established at Cranwell and at various times had been located at Uxbridge, Loughborough, St Athan and Cosford, where it returned in August 1977 after an absence of 23 years. The School is benefiting from the best facilities it ever had and is very much involved in staging major Service and civilian sports events.

The school is responsible for the training of selected personnel as instructors, coaches and leaders in physical, recreational and expedition training.The trainees include Physical Education Officers and RAF and WRAF Physical Training Instructors. A growing function of the School is research into the physical training needs of the RAF.

The training is carried out at Cosford and the two outdoor activity centres at Llanrwst, NorthWales and Grantown-on-Spey in Scotland.

UNIVERSITY OF BIRMINGHAM AIR SQUADRON

The University of Birmingham Air Squadron moved to Cosford early in 1978. The Squadron is commanded by a squadron leader (QFI) with a flying instructional staff of 4 (QFI) officers, and a small administrative staff at the town HQ in Birmingham. Bulldog aircraft are used for the flying training which follows the RAF standard pattern. Ground instruction and other activities take place in the Town HQ which is well situated in Edgbaston, close to the Birmingham University campus.

The Squadron has approximately 35 RAFVR students and 20 officers of various branches on RAF University cadetships; membership extends to students at Birmingham, Aston, Keele and Warwick Universities, with university cadet candidates from local polytechnic undergraduates in addition.

The unit became the first University Air Squadron to be given the honour of being the first such squadron to undertake a summer camp overseas, at RAF Laarbruch, Germany.

PER ARDUA PRO PATRIA

CHAPTER 2

My Liveliest
Guard Duty

*The following is a true report of an incident in which I
was involved whilst serving with No. 82 Squadron
stationed at RAF Watton in Norfolk, circa 1940.*

It was towards the end of November, a bitterly cold night,
with severe ground and air frost and despite the clarity of
the night, there was no flying. That was lucky for some,
but not yours truly, my name had appeared on 'DROs' and
I, with other members of 'B' Flight, had been detailed for
guard duty on that particular night.

I had taken first patrol, which as usual, had proved a routine
exercise, except for the inevitable air raid "stand to". It was
now time for my dreaded 0200hrs to 0400hrs patrol. The
guard corporal had awakened me and I had swallowed my
mug of cocoa. God ! I hated this patrol. Your internal clock
would not let you wake up; there was just that interminable
wish to sleep.

I have left the warm guard room behind me, my five rounds of 'ammo' have been slipped into my Lee Enfield .303 and I now have two hours of patrol. My guard duty takes in one perimeter fence gate, (unlocked), one permanent deep air-raid shelter and six Blenheim Mk. IVs. The ground is hard under my feet, the moon is clear over my head and Blimey, is it ever cold!

I have been into guard duty now about 30 minutes, all is quiet except for the usual sounds of a crisp winter night, the odd owl hoots, a train puffs its way past the far side of the airfield perimeter. Suddenly I am brought to a standstill, was that a glimmer of light in the nose bay of No. 387? It couldn't be! I'm sure it is! There! again – look, a glimmer in the bomb aimer's window, it must be a trick of the light, of course it is. Now I am nearer No 387, there is not a sound, my mouth is very dry, and suddenly I am not as cold as before. I'm nervous – No I'm not, I'm dead scared! There is a light in the bomb aimer's window and it keeps moving about. Who in the hell can it be in there this time of the morning? The aircraft is serviceable, but there is no flying tonight. Maintenance Flight and "B" Flight are off duty, so who the devil is it?

I move stealthily towards the aircraft. I must be mad; I'm sure I can hear whispered voices. My throat and mouth are now bone dry, my knees feel a little weak and suddenly my feet are cold. I walk to the aircraft entry hatch and listen... A shuffling noise; no lights, no voices, just this shuffling noise! What can it be? The aircraft entry hatch is open. What do I do? What do I do?

PER ARDUA PRO PATRIA

I try to compose myself, and find it very difficult. I call.

"Who's there?"

No reply. The shuffling stops, the only sound now is a terrible thumping in my chest, accompanied by a clammy feeling over my whole body. I call again.

"Who's there? Show yourself!"

Not a sound, even the train has passed from earshot. Am I dreaming?

This is not happening to me! Moving to the aircrew entry hatch, I muster all my courage, put one 'up the spout' and call – in what I think is a commanding voice

"Come on! Let's be having you! I know you are in there!"

Deathly silence. I'm sure my heart is coming through my chest. God, I wish I were near a latrine, I feel as sick as a pig!

"This is your last chance! Come on out or I fire!"

How funny! Fire at who? Fire at what? I cannot see a damned thing anyway!

Suddenly there is a movement and a whispered voice.

"Don't shoot! Don't shoot Guv. Give us a second or two. I'm coming out. Don't shoot Guv!."

Well, at least our intruder is no German – his voice rings pure Cockney! I wait a few seconds listening to the shuffling of feet and materials rustling.

"Don't shoot Guv! I'm on my way."

A few more seconds and I am confronted by a fellow in army uniform – well, most of his uniform anyway! He is wearing his cap and shirt and overblouse but no trousers or boots.

"What the ****ing hell do you think you are doing in there?" I demanded of him. "I suppose you are from the army camp over yonder."

"Well... yes... sort of, Guv... But it's not quite as simple as that..."

Nothing could be simple with this find. What on earth was I going to do? Call out the guard? Give a blast on my whistle? Should I fire a round?

Then came the explanation of his "not so simple" comment as behind him there suddenly appeared in the torchlight, a partially clothed WAAF!

PER ARDUA PRO PATRIA

"Didn't fink you'd find us in 'ere Guv," said the soldier. "Sorry about this, you won't put us on a fizzer, will you Guv? Honest Guv, we aint done no 'arm."

What in heavens name was I to do now? If I let them go, they may report me. If I turn them in there will be a court martial to face. Why did I have to find them!

My chest was beginning to pound again!

"Get yourselves dressed and be b**** quick about it or I'll have you both in the guardhouse." I said.

After what seemed an eternity, the offending couple jumped down from the aircraft reasonably attired.

"Now," I said, "Not a sound and follow me..."

I retraced my earlier steps to the perimeter fence gate and checked to ensure it was unlocked.

"Both of you clear off through there and heaven help either of you if word of this incident is leaked out!"

They were gone in a flash and I returned to my guard duty, I was not perspiring so much now, my heart was not pounding so fast, only three quarters of an hour to go, roll on bed-time!

Postscript

The following notice was seen on the NAAFI noticeboard
five days later:

FOUND (IN NOSE BAY OF 387)
LADY'S GOLD PLATED WRIST WATCH
APPLY SGT I/C 'B' FLIGHT

I don't think anyone ever claimed it....

CHAPTER 3

A Test Flight

It was early in 1942 that, together with several hundred of my contemporaries within the RAF, we were hustled aboard the French luxury liner *Louis Pasteur* for transportation to Canada. Although unaware at the time, we were all to become part of what was to be known as "The Commonwealth Air Training Scheme". Because of unsuitable conditions existing in England at that time the training of RAF aircrew was moved to such places as Rhodesia, Canada and the USA.

It became my lot to be posted to No.36 SFTS (Service Flying Training School) at a small outpost named Penhold, some ten or twelve miles from the city of Red Deer, a small town on the prairies in the province of Alberta. Number 36 SFTS was a pilot training school to familiarise aircrew with the handling of twin engine aircraft so enabling their onward promotion to Bomber Command.

We were equipped with Airspeed Oxford Aircraft, of wood and skin construction fitted with two Cheetah X engines. Whilst not a very robust construction they were ideal for their task and flew constantly for many hours with only routine inspection. The major overhaul of the Oxford was executed every 240 flying hours at which time engines were removed and stripped down and the airframe was thoroughly examined for stress fracture, major examination and the incorporation of special modifications.

All inspections including D/I (Daily Inspections) were carried out in special heated hangars during the winter months as blizzard conditions existed and temperatures could drop to 60 degrees below zero giving 92 degree frost! I can assure you there were many unusual and freak accidents when final adjustments were made in the arctic conditions that existed on the tarmac engine tuning pads.

To enable flying to take place in winter months, a fleet of tractors and massive rollers constantly compressed the snow on the runways, so enabling aircraft to make reasonably safe landings and take-offs. The Flying School comprised one Maintenance Wing and three flights, A Flight, B Flight and C Flight, an administration wing and a hutted encampment comprising Headquarters, Officers quarters, NCO and other ranks quarters, dining rooms, Chapel, NAAFI and Canteen. All these respective units were of wooden structure and each surrounded by a huge moatlike ditch to absorb melting snows in the spring of each year.

Although perhaps not relevant to this story I have included this foreward to give a basic insight into conditions at the School.

As I recall, it was in the January of 1943 that I, as a Jnr NCO Fitter E (Engine Fitter) was called upon to fly with an aircraft that had just completed a 240 hour major overhaul. All work had been completed, a daily inspection carried out and the aircraft cleared and signed as airworthy. A qualified pilot instructor had been allocated to flight test the aircraft and as technical NCO in charge of overhaul and daily inspection I was appointed to fly with the aircraft as flight test engineer.

In cooperation with the pilot it was our joint duty to fly the aircraft on a given course and to check all systems e.g. instruments, flaps, undercarriage, stall checks, fuel consumption, oil pressures, oil temperatures, air speed indicator, cabin heating circulation etc.,etc. As the first flight of the day the pilot also had instruction to carry out a full daily weather check. Prior to take-off the pilot had been handed a poor weather forecast by our station meteorological office and a suitable flight plan had been briefed to avoid the bad weather.

After executing all pre-flight checks we taxied to our relevant take-off position, awaited green light clearance from the flight control tower and made a normal though somewhat bumpy take-off. Undercarriage was raised and locked, flaps set and trimmed, our flight path schedule was set and settled down for a routine test flight. The pilot was in constant touch by R/T with the control tower and having reached 3,000 ft., we made several instrument checks and found all to be well. Having satisfied ourselves that all instuments were functioning and flying controls were satisfactory the pilot informed me that he wanted me to switch off the port engine at a given signal and that he would fly for one minute using only the starboard engine. After relevant control adjustments the engine was duly switched off and the necessary exercise executed. All went well and a similar exercise was executed for the starboard engine. We exchanged the thumbs up sign and then I became very apprehensive as the pilot informed me he was going to execute the stall test.

I must be quite honest at this stage and say that the term "stall test" puts me into a cold sweat and it is an exercise I would prefer not to be associated with. For the uninitiated, a stall test comprises a very clever trimming exercise by the pilot, followed by a steady climb and the throttle lever gradually closed until the aircraft loses momentum, both engines stall and the aircraft drops out of the sky. If the nose drops first, control is regained in a reasonable space of time with a good pilot, if you side slip, things become a little more difficult, but when you drop out tail first... a short prayer, a firm grip on your seat and the greatest confidence in your pilot are all that will help you through this most devastating of all air tests.

We made an excellent recovery from our stall test and the pilot in his exhilaration decided to "shoot up" a few fir trees to relax himself and it was agreed we would make for home. Our joint exhilaration was short lived, however, when we discovered that our compass had become unserviceable and the pilot was having some difficulty contacting base. Releasing my harness I walked aft to midships and put my head up into the astrodome. I could observe that the R/T aerial had come adrift from its mounting point at the forward staff and was lashing about dangerously close to the aircraft tail/rudder assembly.

I informed the pilot of the situation and he in turn told me that all communication with base had been lost. He then pointed to the compass, the needle of which was flailing in all directions, gave me the thumbs down followed by a look of complete bewilderment. After our various air tests and a series of aerobatics neither of us had a clue as to our whereabouts. All we knew was that we were flying over a densely wooded area near some foothills. The weather had closed in, a strong wind had risen and visibility was decreasing rapidly.

Meanwhile, the compass was doing everything except function in a normal manner and to make matters worse it started to snow. Fortunately, our fuel situation was quite good and we had several more hours of daylight, but the problem was to discover where we were and how to get back to our airfield...

The pilot worked frantically to make the radio operate, but without success and we had to agree we were hopelessly lost. The compass did nothing but completely confuse us and the snow was now falling quite heavily.

DENNIS WILTSHIRE

We worked on several theories to help us try to obtain a bearing on our return flight, but everything seemed against us. The visibility problem was now quite serious and we were forced to gain some height because of the ever increasing density of the trees and undulating terrain. The pilot had by now become extremely concerned for our safety and I must admit I was more than anxious to be back on *terra firma*. The situation deteriorated rapidly, visibility in the storm was almost zero, ice was building up on the wing leading edges, oil pressures were rising and there was still no compass or radio contact. The pilot decided to climb up to try and lift out of the storm, but thoughts went to the conservation of fuel plus the fact conditions were not improving.

At this stage of the proceedings the altimeter was constantly fluctuating in its readings and the pilot confirmed that this was due to the constantly changing terrain beneath us.

We were lost, we were cold and we were now quite concerned, everything seemed to have turned against us. There was now almost a complete "white out", visibility was zero, the D/F compass was dancing madly, our fuel was down to one quarter capacity. I was nervous to a point of feeling quite sick, the pilot was intensely worried and we were going precisely nowhere.

The pilot suggested I move midships to the wireless operator's desk and harness myself into that position thus enabling me to make an occasional visit to the astrodome to view what was now an impossible situation.

The pilot signalled to me to ensure that I was safely harnessed into my radio operator seat and then he indicated that he was going to take the aircraft down.

I am certain that my internal anatomy went through a changing process: my heart was in my mouth, my stomach was near my boots, I think one can summarise the situation by saying I was now scared stiff! Although I could not read his mind, the pilot appeared full of self-confidence, he made a quick survey of all the instruments, gave the aircraft a few degrees of flap, lowered the undercarriage and started to edge the control column forward.

I was rigid in my seat, I felt terribly sick, looking forward at nothing except a blanket of white, no trees, no hills, no grass, nothing except a white blob – it was terrifying. It seemed never ending, down, down, down, down into nothing. When was it going to end, how was it going to end? The pilot throttled back as far as it was safe to do, down, down, down, how much further and into what?

I felt a sharp crack beneath my feet, the undercarriage had hit something, the pilot pulled the aircraft up, he had felt it also. On, on, on, down, down, then another crack beneath my feet.

Then it happened... it was as if an unseen hand pulled the aircraft down. The wooden propellors disintegrated, perspex screens and windows splintered everywhere, I was thrown forward and downward in my harness, the pilot slumped forward in his harness and the whole aircraft was torn asunder tilting first to port then to starboard. Tree branches tore through the frail canvas and wood structure and the engines screamed to a point of seizure. There was utter confusion, wood, canvas, pieces of tree, snow, perspex and a terrible biting cold wind all around; oil, hydraulic fluid, blood and the most dreaded of all smells... petrol.

I was in a complete state of shock. My harness had kept me secure but my hands and face were scratched and torn by the pieces of flying perspex and wood from the fuselage and trees. The aeroplane had come to rest at the most obtuse angle, I was literally hanging in my harness unable to witness anything outside except masses of snow and green trees. I called to the pilot who was in his harness but slumped over the control column with both arms hanging limply in front of him. I again called to the pilot and receiving no reply, realised I had to do something, no matter what our position.

I think I began to panic, the pilot looked in a bad way, I was suspended by my harness and could not put my feet on anything solid. It was freezing cold and there was that constant smell of petrol. I glanced at the co-pilot's seat which the pilot had told me to vacate. It had been torn from its mountings and a broken tree branch had penetrated the aircraft just about where I would have been seated.

I struggled to free myself, completely forgetting the harness quick release buckle and I began to swear profusely. I screamed for help (I have many times since wondered why) and I truly began to lose my nerve.

PER ARDUA PRO PATRIA

A chance glance at the pilot brought me to my senses again and I realised I had to do something quickly and on my own. I wedged my feet into the airframe superstructure, took my weight by holding a tree branch that had penetrated the aircraft above my head and pressed the harness quick release button. Nothing! I kicked and screamed and pressed and twisted the harness quick release...

The next thing I recall I had fallen forward and was wedged between the co-pilot's seat and the dual control column. I looked up to see blood dripping onto my face and I thought "Oh, God now what have I done!" I had not done anything, the blood was dripping from the face of the pilot but I could not see what injury he had received.

I managed to free myself from my predicament and in so doing, saw from the instrument panel that all electrical switches were in the "ON" position and main power was "ON". I switched "OFF" all the switches I could see and touch and was again terrified by the smell of petrol. I still do not realise how I managed it , but I did manage to stand in a reasonably upright position, lifted the pilot's head to see a severe gash above his right temple. Without giving the matter sufficient thought, I released his harness safety control and the two of us crashed down only to be pinned between the two control columns. Fortunately I fell uppermost so was able to extricate myself and be of some assistance to the pilot.

I can only assume that in the initial crash the pilot must have knocked himself unconscious, for after his second fall with me he regained consciousness and was able to converse with me. He complained of terrible head and neck pain and told me he felt terribly sick. Between us we extracted ourselves from the cramped positions we found ourselves in and lay for a while, not on the floor of the aircraft but on the port side of the aeroplane which proved to be the flattest horizontal position available. After gaining my second wind, I scrambled toward the tail end to open the first aid hatch and retrieve the Red Cross Kit stored inside. Using the contents to the best of my ability I cleaned the pilot's head wound, applied some sterilised coagulant and dressed the wound with a bandage. As he had obviously suffered a mild concusssion, I was dubious about him taking analgesics so made no attempt to offer them. As for myself, with the aid of a polished metal mirror supplied with the first aid kit, I managed to remove several pieces of perspex that had penentrated my head and face and cleaned the wounds with Surgical Spirit.

The storm had increased in intensity and despite our warm clothing we were both feeling terribly cold. We did at least have some protection from the bitterly cold wind, but the snow penetrated every available orifice. Although shocked, freezing cold and with slight injuries we thought seriously about food and warm drinks, but thinking was about as far as we were able to proceed. We discussed our predicament and confirmed that all necessary action and precautions had been taken then we tried to make some plan of campaign. We were both quite weak and in a state of shock, cold, hungry and very weary, to make any plans was out of the question, in the first place we were unaware of our surroundings, we were quite unfamiliar with the terrain and above all we had absolutely no idea where we were or even how far we were from any type of assistance.

The pilot insisted he was tired and wanted to sleep, but I recalled in the distant past someone had told me never to let a patient sleep if he had suffered a blow to the head, so I constantly thought of all things we should do in order to keep the pilot awake. As we clambered about taking pieces of wood and canvas from one place to keep out the cold wind from other places, the pilot suddenly looked me full in the face, smiled and said,

"S and R."

I was quite confused, was it the blow to his head, was he becoming delirious? "S and R" what was he talking about? what was he trying to say? and why was he smiling?

"S and R," he said again. "The S and R beacon, was it working?"

It was the pilot's perogative to think of such things; it had not even crossed my mind. The search and rescue beacon should operate automatically in the event of a crash, I had not even considered it in all the confusion.

"Oh God," I muttered to myself, "please let it be working!"

I looked toward the tail section, or rather what was remaining of the tail section, quite honestly not knowing in the least what I expected to see. I knew where the equipment was fitted but not being an electrician and not ever having any technical reason to handle or maintain the beacon I was quite unfamiliar with it.

I was informed by the pilot that if the beacon was operating it would be emitting a small red intermittent light and a combined bleep signal. We both looked and listened, but with everything considered we were unlikely to know our situation without venturing outside the aircraft. This exercise gave way to considerable thought and planning as we were, at this stage, quite unaware of the situation outside the remains of our aeroplane. The wound dressing I had applied to the pilot's head was showing signs of blood permeating through so, rather than disturb the existing dressing,I placed a pad of cotton wool over the wound area and applied a second dressing. (In those days I was not terribly adept at First Aid). The pilot said he felt quite "groggy" so, placing my parachute pack in the most suitable space I could find, I suggested he rest and use the parachute as a head rest.

The entry/exit door which was positioned midships, aft of the wing trailing edge, had been torn from its hinges, so venturing forth, I started my search for the S and R beacon. The doorway was now at floor level, the aircraft having come to rest on its port side so it was now a question of what lay beneath the doorway and could I get out?

On looking around I came to the conclusion that we had come down in a densely wooded area and that we, or rather the aircraft, was suspended in the trees some feet from the ground. It was bitterly cold and I felt quite nauseated, but we had to do something... Exactly what, I was not quite sure.

Protecting myself against the outside weather conditions as best as as I was able, I put on my sunglasses and proceeded to venture outside to establish the condition of our S and R beacon. A casual glance through the astrodome orifice (the plastic astrodome was no longer in position) showed me that the tail frame unit and tailwheel had separated from the aircraft and lay at a crazy angle some feet away from the aeroplane. Somehow I had to get to the tailframe unit, for that was where the S&R beacon was housed. The snow had eased off a little, but the biting wind tore at my lacerated face as I peered out through the astrodome and eased my body through the vacant orifice. As I climbed through, the light wooden structure disintegrated under my weight, I lost my balance and fell headlong into deep snow and broken pine trees. Fortunately no damage to myself ensued, although I could see in the snow that my facial injuries were bleeding and my sunglasses had fallen somewhere among the debris (the significance of losing my sunglasses will become apparent later).

With extreme difficulty I managed to find my footing, but I was freezing cold, feeling very sick and terribly alone in the world. I tried my utmost to reach the tailplane unit but everything seemed against me; the trees lashed at my face, the cold was intense, the wind penetrating and under the circumstances movement was almost impossible. I extricated myself from the deep snow as best as I was able, but walking was out ot the question without snow shoes or something similar. A glance at my wristwatch told me daylight was coming to a close and the prospects of a night under those conditions did not exactly fill me with confidence.

The tail unit was so near and yet so far, I thought of the energy required to reach the objective and wondered was it all worth the effort? I realised I was sinking into a bad frame of mind and that my morale was at a low ebb, but I wanted to be able to tell the pilot I had found the beacon. I struggled relentlessly and got precisely nowhere, I was infuriated and completely demoralised. It was no longer snowing but it was becoming dark. As I rested for a moment to regain my breathing momentum I thought I heard a sound. Yes there was a sound, a strange little squeak, it was impossible to ascertain its whereabouts. I listened, I felt a little warmer now (fear plays strange tricks with one's metabolism). Yes there was definitely some small creature near me somewhere, "Squeak, Squeak, Squeak", so regular it was uncanny, so rhythmic, so constant. Then things fell into place, the darkness was almost upon us and looking at the tail section I could now plainly see an intermittent light flashing. The S&R beacon was functioning, the little squeak bleeped regularly with the amber light as it flashed.

"Thank God," I thought,"Someone now knows of our plight and will be taking all necessary steps to find us."

I do not know to this day how I managed to get back inside the fuselage, my fingers were numb with cold, I could barely lift one foot in front of the other and with the darkness and bitter cold to contend with I became completely exhausted. I awoke to find myself near the pilot. We had obviously fallen asleep with exhaustion and I had awakened to total darkness and a screaming bitterly cold wind. I looked at the pilot, he was very pale, but from the appearance of his head dressing the bleeding had stopped. I unzipped his flying jacket a few inches and inserted my hand inside, thank heavens his body was warm, so I hurriedly closed his jacket and covered him with a canvas sheet that had appeared from somewhere in the aircraft during the crash, all very neatly folded and tied. Visions of hot drinks and heaped plates of food passed through my mind. We were both cold, hungry and exhausted, but the most wonderful of all was that we were both alive.

The next 36 hours were cold, miserable and uneventful. The pilot was conscious, his wound had stopped bleeding and we were unbelievably cold and hungry and although we saw nothing distinctly, we heard visits from some form of wildlife, but we did the most obvious thing and stayed quiet. As I stated earlier I had lost my sunglasses during the early stages of our accident and the past day had seen a passing of the snow storm and a return to clear blue skies. Unfortunately the strong sunlight against the deep virgin snow gave intense brilliant light, not much warmth, but the most penetrating brightness. One can imagine as a result of this, I suffered acute snow blindness for a long period after this incident and the long term effects remain with me to this very day.

It must seem obvious now to most readers, our S&R beacon was our life saver; a rescue party eventually found us after some 48 hours. From comments later passed we were, when found, a couple of dirty, scruffy and deplorable individuals unfit to be seen in an RAF uniform! However we were taken down and returned to our unit by the rescue party, to whom our gratitude will be never ending. I still recall the wonderful station hospital, the beautiful hot baths, the warm food and drinks and the constant care provided for me.

As for the rescue party, the trip down the mountainside, the ambulance, the doctors, the care and attention, the warmth and comfort of being back at our home unit, I can tell you very little of this except the personal comfort I felt. I was blind for almost two months... but alive.

The pilot that endured this unfortunate experience with me was later posted home to join Bomber Command, and despite arranged plans we never made contact again. I myself was later to become member of Bomber Command on my return home.

War is a strange business, and at 75 years of age although I am still here to tell you this story, I have no idea what became of my pilot? Did he survive the war, or was he one of the thousands of casualties of Bomber Command?

PER ARDUA PRO PATRIA

CHAPTER 4

My Final 295

The following depicts a period in my life of which I am not particularly proud. The details will portray my latter serving months in the RAFVR as a Flight Engineer with Bomber Command.

Perhaps before proceeding further I should explain the title of this transcript. To any ex-RAF personnel the title requires no explanation, but to all other readers a 295 is an official Air Ministry document that certifies official leave of absence from duty.

First, I should perhaps give some details of my early days with the RAF, starting a little after my 18th birthday in March 1939.

I reported to the RAF recruiting centre at Pruet Street in the heart of Bristol, after receiving notification that my application to become a member of "The Royal Air Force Volunteer Reserve" had been accepted.

All the necessary formalities were executed: medical history, education details and the infamous medical examination. All requirements were complied with and I was accepted into the force 'A1' medical, aircrew, in accordance with King's Regulations *and* Air Council Instructions.

There followed many months of further medical examinations, educational tests, receiving of kit, drill training, discipline courses – you name it, I was subjected to it! Because of my height (I was 6ft 2 ins in bare feet) it was regretted by the Royal Air Force Board that I was unsuitable for acceptance as a wireless operator/air gunner, but as I had engineering experience, I would be welcomed as a Fitter 11E (aero-engine fitter).

I should add a further note here to explain that my height of 6ft 2ins acquired me the constant RAF nickname 'Lofty' and was the reason for my failure to attain the position of wireless operator/air gunner because the gun turrets of bomber aircraft in the early days of WW2 could not accommodate aircrew over 5ft 10ins in height.

I will not bore you with the details of the following three years, which I spent in England, Scotland and on overseas duties with Fighter Command, Flying Training Command and Bomber Command.

On return to England from overseas duties, I submitted an application to re-muster from Ground Engineer to Flight Engineer Aircrew. After all the usual Air Board procedures, further training, further medical examinations and

48 ·

conversion to flying training, I attained my wing and was posted to an active heavy bomber squadron as a Flight Engineer, part of a seven member crew of a Lancaster Bomber aircraft.

Our crew of seven comprised:

Leslie (Pilot; 'Skipper')

Reg (Navigator; 'Maps')

Jim (Bomb Aimer; 'Bomber')

Nick (Rear Gunner; 'Tail-end Charlie')

Tom (Mid-upper Gunner; 'Piper')

Fred (Wireless Operator; 'Nosy')

Dennis (Flight Engineer; 'Lofty')

On the particular operation about which I write, we had been briefed, with all the other crews, that our destination was Cologne and that we, as a squadron, were to be part of a three-hundred strong bomber force to attack that city. We were to be preceded en route by aircraft of Pathfinder Force, who would highlight the target area.

As always on a mission, we, the crew of "G" George, were anxious, alert and apprehensive. The 'crew wagon', a Bedford 2-ton truck, with drop tail-board and canvas hood, took us to our aircraft and with Mae Wests, 'chutes, etc, we clambered aboard our aircraft and, with a little banter, took up our respective positions. As Flight Engineer, I shared the cockpit (flight deck) with the skipper; the navigator and bomb aimer were at their stations and the respective gunners to their positions.

The skipper and I went through our respective pre-flight checks, fuel cocks open (or closed) as appropriate, main engine switches 'OFF' – all the usual routine. We were given the all clear to 'START' – each engine in turn bursting into life, over-rich combustion gasses belching from the exhaust stubs, the earth seeming to tremble into life with us.

It is pitch black outside, the navigator has his map table illumination 'ON'. There is very subdued light from the instrument panels. We can see the various ground crew struggling to pull away the 'trolley accs' (starting battery trolleys).

The pilot, in turn, opens the throttle of each engine: No.1… No.2… No.3… No.4… he looks at me; I look at him. RPM OK, thumbs up, radiator shutters 'OPEN' oil pressure steady, thumbs up and so through the whole pre-take off procedure, the A.S.I., the artificial horizon levels up from its drunken position. There is that ever present odour in the kite: a mixture of 100 octane fuel fumes, new rubber, exhaust gasses, hot engine oil accompanied by constant shaking and shuddering, engines roaring. A quick check of the boost gauges. Has the pitot head cover been removed? Damned if I can see. The NCO i/c ground crew thrusts the Form 700 at the pilot to sign (a Form 700 is the official flight and technical clearance to confirm that the aircraft was serviceable for flying when handed over to the pilot from technical ground crew).

There goes the Green Aldis Light for 'G' George (The Aldis Light is a hand-held signal lamp used by flying control to signal either green (OK), red (STOP) or white (HOLD). At some squadrons, Very Pistols fired coloured flares.

The pilot eases the throttles forward, he sets the elevator trim tabs, stick forward, stick backward, left foot forward, right foot forward, a rap on the compass glass. My eyes are flitting from gauge to gauge, boost pressure gauges, fuel gauges, oil temperature gauges, oil pressure gauges, air pressure, hydraulic pressure. The gyros are spinning, all is now alive on "G" George; the whole aircraft shudders and rattles as if it will fall to pieces.

A wave from the pilot signals 'chocks away' to the remaining ground crew outside; a glance at me from Les (our pilot), a wink and a thumbs up – I return a thumbs up and the skipper releases the brakes. The throttles are gradually opened, the propeller pitch controls at their selected positions, both the pilot and I cast a steady glance over the instrument panels and the Lancaster rolls forward. Three of the squadron are already airborne and now we have left dispersal and are at the end of the runway ready for take-off.

Again the green Aldis lamp for "G" George, a few mutterings on the R/T then the crescendo of our four Merlin engines deafening all other sounds as the skipper selects through the gate for 'TAKE-OFF' on all four throttle levers. The pilot concentrates on his take-off procedures, flaps are set and the propeller blades slap at the cold night air as I firmly hold the throttle levers at 'TAKE-OFF' position.

"Flaps set, wheels up," I repeat each command in turn to the pilot. The instruments each dance to their respective tune, RPM, boost pressure, altimeter, compass, red lights go out, green lights come on.

We are airborne – all 65,000lbs of us – including a little over 2,150 galls of 100 Octane fuel and four 5000lb bombs. The fact that we are airborne in itself brings sighs of relief!

The squadron 'groups up' and we head for the coast to position ourselves with our contemporaries ready for the onslaught ahead of us.

We have 'grouped up' and after a long incident-free journey are nearing our target area. It is a dark night, no moon and a little broken cloud some thousand feet below. R/T silence is being maintained with only our own aircraft R/T intercom 'ON'. From the mid-upper gunner and pilot almost simultaneously comes word "Pathfinders ahead!"

I look ahead of the aircraft to see a pale orange glow in the sky. The gunners have fired off a few rounds previously, to ensure satisfactory operation of the guns; we each now in turn confirm our readiness for action and position ourselves accordingly. At this stage of the proceedings, my stomach is in knots. I feel terribly sick, long to be going home to base, and find extreme difficulty in repeating 'The Lord's Prayer' to myself. The orange glow ahead has now turned red, our Pathfinders have done a wonderful job (as always) and the target is well illuminated. The glow now pinpoints other aircraft flying with us, aircraft which we know are there, but have been unable to see because of the darkness.

There is a sudden burst of gunfire from the rear guns.

"Bloody Hell!"

"Sorry, Skip', I thought I saw a fighter."

"Don't think, look! You'll have one of ours down in a minute."

We move ever nearer the target zone; the red glow changes in colour as the first Lancs in drop their green flares to keep the target illuminated. I can see the flashes as the first 5000 pounders fall on the target zone.

Now things are livening up; searchlights are beginning to pierce the darkness; flash bolts are being hurled into the sky to illuminate our presence.

The navigator, in a calm steady voice calls,

"Three minutes to ETA" (estimated time of arrival) followed almost immediately by the bomb aimer.

"Keep her as she is skip, I have greens and reds straight ahead."

We are now feeling the blast effect from the ack-ack shells. We are all at our respective tasks: the bomb-aimer at his window, the navigator at his charts, complete with his shaded light and curtains drawn. The skipper and myself are in almost total darkness, apart from the occasional flash of moving searchlights; Les has his eyes fixed out to our port side, mine to starboard.

Necessary adjustments are executed after sign language to each other. The pilot makes various left and right deviations to our set course, as both searchlights and ack-ack shells become more numerous.

"Bomb doors open," comes the bomb-aimer's call and the whole aircraft seems to want to fall apart as the skipper operates the bomb door lever with his left hand.

I am feeling pretty awful now, I always feel sick over the target, but this time I am in a cold sweat and feel very light-headed. The skipper almost screams at the bomb-aimer.

"For Christ's sake, Jim, hurry up. What are you doing?"

There is a very pregnant pause, then in a voice so calm and collected that I want to scream, Jim, the bomb-aimer, says,

"Left... Left... Left... right a little... steady... Bombs gone!"

The aircraft seems to take-off for a second time as the weight of the bombs is released. All of us are still looking in every possible direction for fear of collision with another of the 300 aircraft out there in the darkness.

The bomb doors close and the skipper makes a steep turn for home, but we are now in the thick of a heavily defended area. The blast of anti-aircraft shells rocks us continuously and tracer shells, bomb bursts and screaming shells are everywhere. Our 5000 pounders burst below us. It is like Dante's Inferno!

I am frozen in my seat. The skipper completes his turn for the home run. This in itself is a major operation. The pilot is flying almost blind and is negotiating a manoeuvre with several dozen other aircraft making the same move.

Something crashes through the perspex window behind me. It screams past my head and buries itself in the cockpit floor; there is a sickly smell of burning and phosphorous. I release my harness, leap from my seat, stamp and stamp on the object, finally using the cockpit fire extinguisher on it. The bomb-aimer has, at this stage, been unable to leave his station due to the turn we are negotiating and various other manoeuvres. He suddenly screams.

"Fire! For God's sake my suit's on fire!"

Like anyone else in such a predicament in a confined space, he kicks and scrambles to get away from his window and then quite suddenly he crumples up and is perfectly still.

There is suddenly a stupendous, blinding flash. The whole aircraft thrashes about like a fish in its final throes of life. Something has passed clean through our forward perspex nose window, taking parts of the bomb-aimer's equipment. I think of those famous words we heard in training, "Keep calm... Don't panic..." I wonder if the person who spoke those words has ever been in such a position as this.

I try to struggle into the bomb-aimer's station; the pressure from the ice cold blast of the slipstream now entering the nose section is immense. I put on my oxygen mask, not for oxygen, but to allow me some semblance of normal breathing in the gushing air. The wind tears at my Irvin jacket, debris is everywhere, odd bits and pieces tear at my face – this is an impossible task.

"Skipper," I call on the R/T, "this is bloody hopeless! I can't even stand up!"

There is another explosive crash somewhere aft in "G" George.

"How is Jim?" asks the Skipper

"I can't get near him, but I think he's had it, Skip. He's bleeding from ears, nose and mouth."

With the added assistance from the unbelievable force of the wind coming through the damaged nose, I return to the cockpit to find chaos reigns supreme. There is glass, oil, and various unidentified liquids everywhere. Several

PER ARDUA PRO PATRIA

of the pilot's instruments are now U/S (unserviceable), but he just sits there as calm and collected as is humanly possible under the circumstances. The skipper is always calm; he is a wonderful guy. For a moment our eyes meet; are we both thinking alike? Then he winks and I think there is a hint of a smile, perhaps of encouragement.

"Check the fuel levels, Den. I don't know what the situation is, you tell me."

"I don't know if we have lost any," I mutter, "Poor old George is like a bloody sieve at the moment, holes everywhere."

I am hoping to God we've got enough to get us home. I check the levels of the tanks, open the relevant bleed/transfer cocks and pumps and transfer the 100 octane fuel, as per the normal procedure. If we have lost any of our precious fuel, it is not much.

From here on I am not truly aware of what happened. I do recall the inferno below us at the target area. I remember seeing a Lanc, minus its tail end, with all four engines on fire, hurtling towards the earth. From then on my mind is a blank.

I was told many months later, that I released the harness I had been wearing at my station, pulled off my helmet and started to walk aft. Apparently I was quite oblivious to frantic calls and abusive screams to sit down and I apparently failed to utter even one word or sound. I also failed to negotiate the main spar, which protrudes upward from the deck of the aircraft and fell to the deck, remaining there motionless. The navigator had apparently left his station to assist me, but finding no visible wounds or blood and being unable to obtain any word from me, returned to his table and charts to plot the homeward journey.

I regret that any information from this point is very sketchy. On landing it was confirmed that Jim was dead and I was taken from the kite by ambulance, which had been forwarned of our arrival by Les, our skipper, and I was taken to station sick quarters.

With de-briefing, breakfast, etc, etc, the other lads in the crew lost touch with my treatment. After a mission such as we had endured, plus de-briefing, breakfast and a good sleep, they each had their own problems.

I must impress that all the lads came to pay their respects, but regrettably I was never aware of their presence.

I was in station sick quarters for approximately four days. I learned eventually that I was as much a problem to the crew on their visits as I was to station medical officers. I was diagnosed as having no wounds, no broken bones and no physical disabilities, but I was apparently quite content to remain in bed oblivious of anything and everything. I could not stand or sit. I ate nothing. I drank nothing. I did not seem to understand any spoken word and, despite attempts by all medical staff, nothing would register in my mind.

PER ARDUA PRO PATRIA

A civilian consultant psychiatrist from a nearby hospital was requested to attend the station sick bay. I am unable to confirm this. It was only learned by me many months later, either by letters from my colleagues or from third or fourth hand word of mouth.

My story somewhat changes at this point. I was, it seems, taken to an RAF mental hospital situated at Matlock in Derbyshire. Here, along with many other aircrew types, I was destined to become one of what our RAF colleagues referred to as "a right load of nutters"! For many weeks – I am not sure how long – I do not know what happened to me. My life was just a blank. I did not know then; I do not know now and at almost 80 years of age, I am certain I never shall know. I assure you it is very disconcerting not to be aware of what has happened to part of one's life.

It does appear, however, that when I was receiving some form of treatment at Matlock Hospital, a nurse accidentally knocked a steel dish of medical instruments from a trolley on to the floor. Upon its impact, it seems I sprang to my feet, fell flat on the floor, because of my weak state and was screaming, "There's another poor sod going down, let's get the hell out of here! Look at the flares! Look at the flares! Shoot the bastard down, they're coming closer, for God's sake shoot the bastard down!"

I then collapsed...

What happened with, or to me I do not know, but I do recall coming round. I was in a bed with wonderful snow-white sheets, beautiful soft white pillows, a nurse seated at my bedside in a lovely crisp, blue and white uniform.

"Doctor! Doctor! He's awake, Doctor!"

It was presumably the doctor who spoke to me. He was in white, but his shoulders bore epaulettes bearing "Air" rank.

"Well, Laddie, and how are we today?"

"A little bit confused, sir. No, very confused. Confused, hungry and feeling very weak thank you, sir."

There followed a series of questions, from which I did not make an awful lot of sense. Instruments were inserted in my ears; instruments were put up my nose. He peered into my eyes from all angles, rubber mallets struck me here, rubber mallets struck me there!

For several weeks I was subjected to the most unbelievable set of tests. I do not recall all the details. You must remember this all happened over 50 years ago and I was not exactly in the pink of health. There is one thing I do recall... "E.C.T." – those letters are stamped on my brain, such as it is, and those letters will remain with me forever.

I was taken in a wheelchair through various passages, corridors and lifts, until arriving at a door bearing the letters "E.C.T." For the uninitiated, these letters are the abbreviation of "Electro-Convulsive Therapy." For those readers aware of this treatment 'welcome to the club' – for those not aware,

I fervently hope that you never will become a member of this particular 'club'!

The treatment comprises (at least it did for me for me 50 years ago) a course of regular sessions, where, I was lying flat on a bed having only a rubber mattress and one flat rubber pillow, (no bed linen whatsoever) and wearing only a sleeveless gown tied at the back of the neck. I was placed on the bed and told to remain perfectly still. A nurse checked my heart rate and pulse and checked for the wearing of dentures. A doctor then introduced himself and addressed himself to an item of medical equipment comprising a metal cabinet on castors with various dials and electrical leads mounted upon it. The nurse handed the doctor a small container of gel, into which he placed his gloved finger, removed some of the gel and placed it on my left temple. The procedure was repeated on my right temple. I was then instructed to open my mouth "wide" and a large rubber gum-shield was inserted into my mouth, the gum-shield having a cord attached, which rested on my chest. Two electrical leads with a scissors clamp and rubber pads at the end of each scissors were then connected to the machine and one rubber pad placed on the gel at each of my temples. The doctor proceeded to inject what I now know to be an anaesthetic into my left forearm and I remember little else of that session. I have obviously made it my business to establish what happens after the injection but I truly do not think that the details warrant printing here. The best part of this treatment was a super cup of strong tea fifteen minutes after completion; the personal effects are not a suitable subject for print here.

To bring the story of this part of my life to an end, I should perhaps close with a happy ending. Unfortunately, as we all know, only fairy stories have happy endings, and this is not a fairy story.

In late 1944, when still a patient at RAF Hospital Matlock (known to inpatients as "Hatters' Castle") my service life came to an abrupt end. After many weeks of treatment and many weeks of wearing my hospital uniform, I was requested to attend a Royal Air Force Discharge Medical Board.

I was once more subjected to unbelievable tests, questions, cross examinations by senior medical officers, psychiatrists, neurosurgeons and representatives of the RAF Mental Health Board.

Some weeks after this inquisition I was requested to attend a further medical board; this was quite a different affair. I now had no official RAF uniform (all my kit and uniform had been lost somewhere between my last squadron HQ and the hospital). I was issued with a complete new set of 'hospital blues' – royal blue jacket and trousers, white shirt, red tie and an RAF issue forage cap, complete with badge.

I was invited into the room where the Board had assembled and I was asked to sit down in a beautifully carved wooden chair. Sitting at a long table in front of me were three senior medical officers (I cannot remember their ranks) and three civilians.

Strange to relate, one of the civilians at the table read out from a sheaf of papers "Do you confirm that—?" and he quoted my full name, service number, date of birth, a brief history of my four and a half year service life and ended with "do you agree?"

I confirmed my name, rank and serial number, but at that time I had to admit that the previous years were a complete blank in my mind.

photo courtesy of the *Derbyshire Times*.

The 'Hatter's Castle'

I was then addressed by a Squadron Leader MO (Medical Officer), who read from KRs & ACIs (King's Regulations and Air Council Instructions) what seemed to me to be a load of 'mumbo-jumbo'. He also informed me that the matter would be made clear to me on return to my ward... it was!

Some days later the same MO came to my ward bed and explained that I had served four and a half years as a member of the RAFVR, that I should feel proud that I had served my king and country and that I had an unblemished service record, technical, flying and discipline. He went on to inform me that as from a certain date, I would cease to be a member of "His Majesty's Royal Air Force (VR)" and that arrangements would be made to clear all service documents and transport arranged to take me to my home address at Bristol.

All that was almost 55 years ago. I now find that difficult to believe. There are so many events I recall quite easily, others, of which I have been told but which remain locked somewhere in my mind.

There is no real end to this particular episode in my life. To this day the RAF remains prominent in my mind and I often think of "Skipper" and the 'boys' of 'Hatters' Castle' with its abundance of broken lives.

Almost 25 years later there was to be a repetition of my problem – but that is another story...

PER ARDUA PRO PATRIA

CHAPTER 5

Space Technology "Spin-Off" Benefits

Although of a technical nature, it is hoped that many readers will come to appreciate that many benefits now afforded the general public are as a result of space-technology 'spin-off'.

INTRODUCTION

With the continuing advances in aerospace technology, the "spin-off" benefits increase too. Although man has now set foot upon the moon, sent unmanned probes to Mars and Venus and placed a series of satellites into earth orbit, we have only touched upon the fringe of celestial and interplanetary venture. Yet from those early and what will some day seem to be clumsy attempts, we have, as individuals, gained many assets which affect our daily lives.

It is indeed regrettable that the innumerable persons who denounce the space-programmes as "a waste of money" do not give a little more thought to the space programme as a whole, including the "spin-off" benefits. I cannot and do not disagree that billions of American dollars are spent each year on the space-programmes, but this is American money and it is not for us to criticise how the American tax-payers' money is spent. On the other hand, there are many medical, industrial, scientific and general "spin-off" benefits which are readily available to all who seek them, but again regrettably, we hear all too little of these aspects of the space-programmes.

I have spent a considerable amount of time and effort endeavouring to bring to the attention of the general public the many benefits which they enjoy, both directly and indirectly, as the result of space-technology "spin-off".

I trust all who read this article will at least find it interesting, if not educating and I hope that the information supplied herein will be passed on to the uninitiated.

My grateful acknowledgements are offered to NASA organisations for their cooperation in assisting me with this project.

GENERAL

A computer programme (Cosmic-dissemination) designed to optimise a group of design parameters, has been requested by over 300 different companies throughout the USA. At the Bonneville Power Dam, for example, engineers used the programme to optimise design of control circuitry, while General Foods applied it to optimise the variables in food preparation and produce "consistent" foods. The University of North Carolina has adapted the programme to medical research and public health, to determine where the available funds should best be spent to improve living standards, education and health care in deprived areas. Engineering firms, electronic specialists, chemical and petroleum companies also list among the users of this programme.

A device developed at Langley Research Center called an "underseas pinger" was originally developed for the location of space capsules and test rockets and it has also helped in plotting ocean currents and in tracing the movements of fish. It will be required on certain aircraft that fly over-water routes and used on vessels carrying nuclear and other specialised types of cargo. The device sends out a signal that is picked up by conventional sonar equipment, guiding a search vessel to its location. The pinger is powered by a battery, but the system remains inactive until immersed in water. Other methods for activation of the system can be used. The system, now being manufactured by two small companies, was recently voted one of the year's best 100 inventions.

A particle counter has been developed for Marshall Space Flight Center to monitor air purity in clean rooms where small precise components are assembled and tested. Announcement of this counter has generated requests from a variety of industrial firms across the U.S.A. Several hospitals have shown interest in adapting it for monitoring air cleanliness in operating rooms and intensive care wards. One instrument manufacturer is experimenting with the unit in the hope of developing a similar device for detecting minute flaws in fast moving stock in paper mills.

A cluster of hanging chains has been shown to reduce wind-induced bending oscillations of tall cylindrical antenna masts. The damping system, developed at the NASA Langley Research Center, consists of chains covered with a flexible plastic or rubber sleeve. They are suspended inside a neoprene shroud from the top of the mast and are completely enclosed by the mast structure. In a particular example, the chain damper, which weighed 6kg, increased damping of a tower that weighed 130kg by twenty times. The undamped antenna had a response peak at a wind velocity of 5kt, and at 60kt the damped system showed less vibration than the undamped antenna did at 5kt.

Grease and oils may break down or evaporate at high temperatures and in vacuum, so solid materials are often superior, but standard dry lubricating bearing surfaces, made by a powder metallurgy method, are described in a NASA Tech Brief and a more recent dry, self-lubricating cage material was reported by Lewis Research Center.

The report on the latter material drew fifty enquiries for further information within the first months after the announcement. Potential applications include food processing equipment and textile machinery where contamination from oils and greases cannot be tolerated.

Transducers, developed for measuring the impact of a Command Module during water landings, are being used in the fitting of artificial limbs. The transducer is smaller than a £1 coin and weighs less than 50 grm. The sensing diaphragm is of stainless steel and the whole unit is waterproof. As used in the module, or in the hospital, it will respond to static or dynamic changes in pressures, and is not affected by temperatures between freezing and 120 degrees F.

There are often instances of "negative" transfer, that is when transfer of technology results not in a new product or procedure for the recipient, but in a decision to abandon a proposed effort. Negative transfers are useful in that they generally represent a saving, or redirection, of valuable research time and resources that might otherwise be wasted or utilised inefficiently.

A Baylor University Medical School physiologist, studying dispersal forces of diagnostic dye in the blood stream has reviewed the biomedical literature for reports of interaction of the dispersal forces, and finding little, felt this would be an area for further study. Before he undertook the work he requested the NASA-sponsored Biomedical Applications Team at Southwest Research Institute to make a search of the aerospace literature on the subject. A NASA data bank search was performed using non-biomedical search terms. It revealed that, in fact, this problem had been well studied, but as a physical not medical problem, i.e. liquid flowing through a flexible tube. This search was the basis for the investigator's decision to abandon his plan.

MEDICAL

A sensor developed at the Ames Research Center is smaller than the head of a pin and can be inserted into a vein or artery to measure blood pressure without interfering with circulation.

The probe can be inserted through a standard hypodermic needle, and the doctors have reported that patients felt no discomfort when it was used. A hospital has used the sensor to evaluate implantation of artificial heart valves, and a physician has pointed out that the sensor is small enough to be used for children - even infants - where previous equipment proved insufficiently sensitive if made very small. The original version of the transducer was developed for pressure surveys in wind tunnels, and for the telemetry of pressure data from small, free-flight models.

A NASA contractor at the Mississippi Test Facility has improved on the design of an orthopaedic stretcher. Now licensed for manufacture, it was originally designed to remove a workman from large, deep tanks having access holes of only half a metre in diameter. The stretcher holds the subject essentially in the traction while raising him through the access hold. This suggests usefulness in recovering a trapped miner who may be injured or an injured mountain climber in a difficult-to-reach location. The stretcher features a "scissors" arrangement that permits its two sides to be separated, slipped under the subject, then locked in position. This firm support is of considerable importance in the case of serious injury.

Combinations of sensing devices and advanced electronics provide means of telemetering medical information from moving humans and animals without contact and without interference with normal activities. Since the original development work at Ames Research Center, commercial versions of the devices have become available from several sources. A course of electronics has included the information, and students have been given laboratory projects of building the electronic circuitry. One of the designs for implantation will operate for over 5,000 hours on its self-contained battery. Power drain must be held to a minimum, since the battery that forms the power source is the largest component of the system. The units have been supplied for telemetering electro-cardiograms, electro-encephalograms, impedance pneumograms, blood pressure and electromyograms.

A centrifuge at Ames Research Center was used by a team of medical specialists to reposition a bullet lodged in a man's brain. Removal by normal surgical techniques would have caused blindness or other severe curtailment of his capabilities; leaving it in place would have meant death. The centrifuge, called a "five degrees of motion simulator", was used to apply a force equal to six times that of gravity, in a precisely controlled direction, causing the bullet to move to a portion of the brain where it could be left without serious danger to the patient.

Heart implants, as well as other surgical implants, may be rejected by the body. For this and other reasons, physicians often wish to know the output of blood pumped by the heart, and of any changes which may indicate problems of progress towards recovery. A device called the four-electrode impedance plethysmograph has been developed for the Manned Spacecraft Center, that makes the determination without adding the hazard of injecting a foreign substance into the body; for example, foreign materials would increase the possibility of rejection. The electronic circuitry allows the physician to learn, not only the volume being pumped, but also the change with time and the rate of change with time, These provide early warning signals so that prompt corrective action can be taken.

To better diagnose heart disease, it is necessary to better understand the mechanical actions of the heart. One way to do this is to measure the electrical signals resulting from this heart action, as is commonly done with the electrocardiogram (ECG).

An investigator wished to monitor heart action even more precisely, by measuring electrical signals simultaneously along 15 points and which would not result in heart wall damage upon insertion. The NASA-sponsored Research Triangle Institute Biomedical Applications team explained the problem for an instrument engineer. He designed a 15-electrode probe within an ordinary hypodermic needle. It was fabricated, tested, found satisfactory, and is now in use.

When it becomes necessary to acquire specimens of tissue from the inner ear for medical examination, the outer bony structure must first be removed. This is difficult and time-consuming since the bone must be chipped away and dissolved. A special air-abrasive device was known to NASA and its use was suggested to the investigator at the University of Kansas Medical Center. He tried the instrument and found that it was substantially better than previous techniques for removing bone from the ear and saved considerable time.

The rate of growth of plant and animal tissue can be influenced by the application of electric and magnetic energy usually increased by increasing field intensity. To be able to apply this phenomenon towards development of methods for more rapid healing of injured tissue, a technique for measuring changes in the activities of single cell organisms, as they are affected by electromagnetic fields and currents, is required. A search of NASA literature revealed a report entitled "Biomagnetics: Considerations Relevant to Manned Space Flight", which the requesting researcher at the

University of Missouri considered a good reference source which would be useful in his research programme.

As the hospitalised patient begins to recover and move about the ward, it becomes more difficult to keep constant check on his medical condition. A system to send biomedical data by radio transmission from the patient to the physician would allow the patient some freedom of movement, yet ensure that the physician could be aware of the patient's condition at any time. Researchers at an American Handicapped Person Center wished to know if such a system was feasible under hospital conditions. Data from an unpublished NASA study on radio transmissions under similar conditions were located by a Biomedical Applications Team which indicated that the system was indeed feasible and that commercial equipment was available. Tests have shown the system to be satisfactory.

In evaluating the safety and efficiency of drugs for human use, the effect of a particular drug on the circulation of blood through capillaries is of great importance since they are an integral part of body tissue around them. The present methods for determining capillary circulation are crude and indirect because the capillary vessel may have a diameter less than half of that of human hair. A search of the NASA aerospace literature was made by the Research Institute Biomedical Applications Team, the results of which were helpful to a physiologist in beginning a pilot programme on the solution of this problem at the University of Minnesota.

An endocrinologist needed an implantable instrument to measure small temperature changes of internal organs and cavities in a patient and to transmit this information on a receiver. The instrument had to be implanted for several months with no adverse reaction. A NASA literature search revealed reports on a small temperature telemetry system developed by the Ames Research Center and recently commercialised. The transmitter signals are picked up by a standard FM receiver. The investigator has procured two units; one unit has been implanted in a patient for more than three months with very satisfactory results.

Loss of voluntary control of the urinary function can result from a number of injuries and diseases, and can result in tissue deterioration, and in some cases, kidney damage and death. This condition affects an estimated 15,000 new patients per year in the U.S.A. and is the most frequent cause of death for paraplegics. Current attempts at alleviating this problem have not been wholly successful.

A researcher felt the solution would lie in a simple but reliable, totally implantable, valve device that the patient could control easily. The Research Triangle Institute Biomedical Application Team submitted this problem to NASA Center Scientists in the form of a Biomedical Problem Abstract. A NASA engineer at the Lewis Research Center suggested a valve design based on one he uses for manometer tubes. It can be controlled by pressure and would remain open if it failed so that there would be no blockage of the urinary tract. The valve system has been re-engineered and a prototype constructed. It is now being tested before implantation.

Study of the effects of stress on the normal heart helps to understand strokes and other cardiovascular disease. Researches at the University of Washington were evaluating the effects of two concurrent stress elements, physical effort and heat, and blood oxygen transport. An inclined-plane treadmill was available to provide physical effort stress, but a means of carefully controlling skin blood temperature without interfering with movement was needed. NASA-developed "space underwear", with a temperature-control system, was obtained from NASA by the Southwest Research Institute Biomedical Applications Team and was used by the investigators in successfully completing the study.

In the care and rehabilitation of the severely burned child, it is desirable that biochemical changes in the respiratory tract be monitored as a means of determining the child's overall condition. this may be accomplished to a large extent by monitoring the respirations of the child, but this should not involve touching the child's body or connecting air tubes to his throat, because of the pain and air-way restriction involved.

A respirometer developed at NASA's Ames Research Center appeared to meet the qualifications of the investigators at the Shriners Burn Institute of the University of Texas. A prototype of this respirometer will be made available for evaluation.

Aerospace technology may play a part in reducing radiation hazards for those patients who must be treated with radioactive iodine. An isotope, Iodine 123, may reduce the radiation dose, when used with the proper equipment, by a factor of almost 10,000; the isotope would replace the ractor-produced isotope Iodine 131. Cost of preparation of Iodine 123 had limited its use in diagnosis and treatment, but now an economical method for its preparation has been developed.

INDUSTRIAL

An explosively actuated tube swager developed at the Langley Research Center, can now meet current needs in industry; the device joins two sections of tubing by bonding an exterior metal sleeve to each tube. The swager is actuated by the energy from a 0.22 calibre blank cartridge, and the resulting joint is impervious to liquids and gases and also resists damage from vibration. After firing, a groove is visible in the outer sleeve if a sound joint has been made, providing a quick check of the joint quality.

A new class of organic polymer, with high stability to heat, light and radiation, has been announced from Langley Research Center. A foam ablative material, based on this polymer, is to be tested in the near future; the high heat resistance of the material should offer advantages in ablative shields. In another application, a company is experimenting with the new polymers as a coating for wire in aircraft service, where the combination of strength and resistance to high temperature is the source of interest.

Two recent developments in new materials achieved by NASA's Lewis Research Center are:

1. A new ferromagnetic cobalt base superalloy, which has a high-temperature rupture strength to an order of magnitude (a factor of 10) greater than the strongest magnetic alloys of comparable magnetic properties in use. The new alloy can be used in the construction of electric motors and generators operating at high temperatures.

2. A tungsten fibre-reinforced nickel superalloy that is four times as strong as conventional nickel-base super-alloys. This composite material consists of tungsten fibres enmeshed in a nickel-base superalloy. It successfully utilises the strength of refractory metal fibres to reinforce metals at high-temperature. It will be useful where higher strength or a greater strength-to-density ratio is required in high-temperature systems and components. Examples of potential applications include high-temperature turbine components, such as vanes and coolant tubes also turbine generator components for advanced electrical power system.

Marshall Space Flight Center has designed and put into practice a simple, hand-held lead bending tool for forming the leads of electronic components to precisely fit in the appropriate holes of printed circuit boards. A manufacturing corporation has obtained rights to use of the patented items and has modified the tool to include a lead cutting capability.

Manufacture of the popular air bearings used in precision guidance and controls systems has involved some problems in achieving sufficiently smooth surfaces. Hard-anodised aluminium laps, developed at Marshall Space Flight Center, have now largely solved this problem. These laps have produced scratch-free surface finishes on beryllium four times finer than previously possible and they can be used repeatedly while showing only a fraction of the wear experienced with the older laps made from cast iron, brass or granite. These long-life laps are now commercially available for either bore-type or flat surface lapping.

Tack welding has often been used in the alignment of large work-pieces in preparation for tungsten inert gas (TIG) weld joining. A new approach to this method of manufacture has been the installation of a number of clamps which hold the work pieces in true alignment by means of a thin steel band held in tension through the joint to be welded. These clamps may be adjusted over a large tension range and do not interfere with the welding procedure since each clamp is removed before the weld machine reaches it.

Flat conductor cable has been under investigation for many years and has now reached a highly successful stage of development. these cable forms have been found to offer advantages to electrical system designers by saving weight, space, cost and lead time within excellent reliability and uniform electrical characteristics. Concurrent with development of these cables, a large family of tools, fixtures and test equipment has evolved to advance their preparation, installation and repair.

Mention of a NASA document in a trade publication started a chain of events that led a small firm under contract to the Spacecraft Center to build an instrument for checking the flared ends of tubes. The device, which can be built in other configurations, has a master cone with a thin film of insulation that forms a capacitance with the tube under test. The result, read out on a capacitance meter, show whether the fit is good or faulty. The simplicity of the device makes 100% checking practical. The firm estimates that the NASA document saved as least two days of development time, and required only about an hour of review before it was put to practical use. An American firm has used directly, the design of a special fixture for metallurgical specimens that makes it practical to polish soft specimens by machine. In metallurgical polishing the aim is to obtain an undisturbed surface. With hard metals, this does not pose much of a problem, but with soft materials, a mounting, heavy enough to provide the required inertia, is enough to cause smearing of the metal surface, destroying the structure to be examined. The fixture, developed at AEC's Argonne National Laboratory, was originally planned to solve a problem in polishing uranium, but can be applied to many soft metals.

Electroless nickel plating, a method for depositing a nickel phosphorous alloy without the use of electric current,

PER ARDUA PRO PATRIA

requires special preparation of the surface of the object to be plated, as well as close process control. The coating prevents galling, and makes it easier to solder aluminium and the stainless alloys. Some metals are relatively difficult to process in this manner. For use in the Goddard Space Flight Center programme, a contractor developed methods for electroless plating on several different stainless steels and an aluminium alloy. A Detroit firm has found the process improved the uniformity of plated die cavities reducing the number of rejects. A petrochemical firm is considering the process for stainless steel equipment, and another firm found the method superior to its own proprietary process.

A joining process, developed for NASA for preparing highly accurate, hollow, spherical rotors, has been applied to other types of joints in the electronic industry. The method was developed under Jet Propulsion Laboratory contract to make highly precise spheres. Joining by brazing, fusion welding, of diffusion welding resulted in excessive distortion. In the new process, an undersize insert closes the gap and the joint is filled by electroplating metal into the area, then machining away the excess. Since the process is carried out at room temperature, there is little chance for distortion. The NASA process was sufficiently effective that it has been incorporated into the plant's regular manufacturing procedures.

Compounding of an inorganic paint is a highly specialised task, in which variations in composition, the order in which the ingredients are mixed, and even the nature of the mixing equipment, play an important part. These and other variables need to be considered in relation to the use planned for the paint - the substrate, the method of application, and the nature of the environment against which the paint is to protect. Companies in the field who learned about paint formulation developed at Goddard Space Flight Center are reviewing it with a view to adapting the information to their own needs, and those of their customers.

One of the most trying problems for technicians checking out faulty circuitry has been the identification of degraded components that have not completely failed. The past procedure has been to remove semi-conductor devices from circuitry. An American company has developed its own system and successfully tests semiconductor components in situ at an appreciable saving in technicians' time and component or circuit damage. The firm using it expressed the feeling that the information obtained from a NASA document resulted in a very adequate, quick, qualitative test, found to be satisfactory in a wide range of electronic trouble shooting.

Marshall Space Flight Center has announced three welding techniques that are novel in that they permit a high degree of weld integrity under unusual weld conditions. The Pennsylvania State University College of Engineering and Department of Materials Sciences has adopted these techniques as background material in industrial engineering courses at two levels. The instructor in these courses is convinced that this type of information supplied by NASA is filling a void in the literature.

A compact water-cooled mount for commercial miniature pressure transducers, developed by NASA, permits installation of the transducers in hotter (over 1000 degrees F) and more confined areas than was previously possible. The result is a significant improvement in pressure-sensing capabilities in such locations. A manufacturer of miniature pressure transducers learned of this NASA development and is planning commercial manufacture of the water-cooled mounting.

An improved punch and die set, for fabrication of Centaur vehicles and support equipment has been developed. this tool has the advantage of producing tubing flares that are dimensionally accurate and stronger than those made with conventional tools and also tighter tubing connections. Subsequently, a company developed with its own funds a machine incorporating punch and die. A patent was obtained for the machine and a licence for its manufacture has been granted.

An American contractor to NASA developed a closed-loop temperature controller having higher sensitivity, reliability and power capacity than commercially available units. With a different sensing element, the device can also be used as a low-pressure controller. As a low-pressure controller, it is directly applicable to many automation systems where low-pressure processing requires critical control of fluid feed pressure. The company that developed the controller has included the device in their production line as a solid state temperature switch.

An ultrasonic temperature-measuring device has been incorporated in the production line of a company which developed the device while under contract to NASA. This device determines by measuring the transit time of an acoustic (sound) pulse in a wire sensor or probe inserted into the test environment. It operates on the principle that the speed of sound in a sensor material is a function of temperature, and can function in the extremely high temperatures in the core of a nuclear rocket engine. Unlike thermocouples, no electrical insulation is needed, and the probe can be chosen from a range of suitable alloys. It is stable to shock and vibration, can tolerate high pressures and substantial excess temperatures, and is not limited by past geometry.

A multiple foil gauge has been developed that measures crack growth in materials at cryogenic temperatures - down to 455 degrees F below the freezing point of water. It is used in evaluating structural materials. Measurements with other gauges become difficult or impractical when specimens were immersed in a cryogenic liquid, or when the sample had a curved surface, such as that of a cylindrical pressure vessel. As the crack in the sample widens, the electrical resistance of the assembly increases in linear steps. These gauges were first fabricated for NASA, and the maker subsequently added them to his production line.

Microwaves, used for some time in radar and communication systems, are also effective in detecting tiny fatigue cracks in metals. Cracks as small as a ten-thousandth of an inch are detectable by this method, scientists have found. Contact

PER ARDUA PRO PATRIA

with the part is not necessary, nor is the part damaged. Even complex shapes, such as turbine blades and discs, can be tested by microwaves. The system can measure the growth of a fatigue crack while the sample is under test conditions, and could even be modified for testing in a vacuum.

There are often times in industry when the metal in a component part must be identified, yet it is not feasible to damage the specimen for chemical analysis. A process developed for the Manned Spacecraft Center provides a solution. It is particularly applicable when two batches of metal are mixed, or when it is suspected that some parts are not of the desired alloy. The test is rapid and relatively simple. Two leads are connected, one to the sample to be tested, the other to an electrode dipped into a drop of water on the surface of the specimen. The electrode must not touch the test piece. The voltage generated, its polarity, and any decay characteristics are compared with those from a known sample; if they match, the known and the unknown are of identical composition.

An electromagnetic hammer for use in the fabrication of large boosters, has been designed at Marshall Space Flight Center, that uses magneto-motive force to form metal surfaces to any desired configuration with a finite control not previously possible with conventional mechanical force devices of desired forms or shapes apply controlled pressure to metal workpieces against dies or moulds to achieve precise configurations. The U.S. Maritime Administration borrowed such a device from NASA and used it effectively in one quarter inch deck plates at a Middle East shipyard.

The foregoing are but a few of the many hundreds of space technology "spin-off" benefits, now accepted on a world-wide basis into the fields of medicine, industry and sociology. Artificial heart technology, environmental technology, life detection systems, material sterilisation, provisioning of medication to sick children, improved welding techniques - the list is formidable and increases daily. Many of us living today are considerably indebted to the skill and crafts of the space technicians.

CHAPTER 6

A Volunteer Again

After fifty happy and wonderful years of marriage I spent the last many months of our time together nursing my dear wife through a terrible and traumatic illness. She was eventually taken from me in 1994 and since then I have found my life empty and void. Unable to cope with the loneliness and uncanny stillness of our home, I started to make inquiries as to what type of voluntary work I might be best suited to.

A chance remark by a long standing member of "The Hospital League of Friends" grasped my attention and after a few informal inquiries I obtained a membership form, completed same and forwarded it to the membership secretary with my fee and in no time at all, I was initiated into the ranks of volunteers, able to make my own choice of work and I have not looked back since.

For the peace of mind both the hospital and the League have afforded me, I have bequeathed a park bench, in memory of my dear wife, which is now sited at Haven Ward where she was nursed and cared for most professionally until her life was taken on 13th.December 1994. To the League I have devoted my time, to enable me to bring some relief both to the patients and to the staff of Barry House at the hospital.

My dear friend, mentioned in the dedication of this booklet, urged me to write this publication, to throw some light on the work of "The League of Friends" and to stop further vegetation of my brain.

Since taking up my duties with the League at Barry House, I have found myself to be committed to helping the sick, frail and injured patients who are in their twilight years. I have found my duties to be more than satisfying; they have been interesting, informative, absorbing, at times humorous and at other times devastatingly sad.

The patients, bless them, what can one say to them? They are the citizens of this country, who have carried us through two World Wars, a devastating General Strike, they have worked hard all their lives to give us a new generation and now, sickness, dementia and old age have captured them in their nets.

The nursing staff, what adjectives describe these modern day Florence Nightingales, young, vibrant, eager, keen, wholesome, hardworking, tireless, I think that is a sufficient tribute to a respected group of professionals, whose counterpart of some sixty years ago worked under devastating conditions for a salary of twenty five pounds per year!

The doctors, how does one begin to describe this band of professional intellectuals. I could say so much but knowledge and modesty prevail.

The domestic staff, again, what can one say? The forgotten army who constantly clean and wipe and wash and mop and brush, what would every ward be without its domestic staff. They are the unsung necessity of every hospital, sharp, aggressive and belittled, but where would the patients be without them?

Compared to the majority of League members I am a comparative newcomer, but like most active members I take my duties seriously and attend the hospital as frequently as time will permit. Although seventy five years of age, time is at a premium for me, since the death of my dear wife, I have become a sick visitor for both the Royal Air Forces Association and the Soldiers, Sailors and Airmen Families Association besides my duties for the League.

As I have said earlier in this saga, life in the hospital is a mixture of happiness and sadness and I hope you will find the following anecdotes from hospital life, interesting if nothing else.

Incidentally, if you are at this stage wondering what my duties are at the hospital, perhaps I should inform you that to both staff and patients I seem to have become affectionately known as "The Tea Man".

Several days a week I do, with other members of the League, serve tea and coffee to the patients of Barry House.

Barry House is an annexe of the hospital reserved for the aged and infirm of this generation. It comprises four wards and a day hospital; the day hospital and Wards 1 and 2 are on the upper road level, Wards 3 and 4 on the lower road level. My duties take me to all four of the wards but refreshments at the day hospital are served by the hospital staff.

The few hours that I spend each day at my duties bring me into contact with all members of staff and visitors. I can assure you life is never dull and I hope what follows will give you some insight into the life of "The Tea Man of Barry House".

Note: to avoid any personal reflections, all names quoted henceforth are purely fictitious so avoiding any embarrassments.

My first story involves an elderly female patient, confined to her bed, and also a young trainee nurse; we will call the patient Gladys and the nurse Topsy. I approach Gladys' bed , pushing my tea/coffee trolley and remark, "Your usual?" to which Gladys replies with the sweetest of smiles "Yes please, dear, you are very kind." Gladys hands me an Oxo cube from her bedside locker and I return to my trolley and commence to prepare a cup of Oxo.

PER ARDUA PRO PATRIA

I am being watched closely by a nurse who now has her eyes riveted on the cup, the Oxo and the boiling water. As I stir the Oxo, Nurse Topsy says, "Whatever are you doing?" I reply that I am preparing Gladys a cup of Oxo, to which the nurse replies, with a look of astonishment on her face, "You're making her gravy! And she is going to drink it!"

Both Gladys and I look at each other, look at the cup of Oxo, then peer at Nurse Topsy and together say, "Not gravy, but a cup of Oxo."

By now poor Topsy is flabbergasted and goes to great lengths to explain that she makes her gravy with Oxo. After remonstrating with the nurse for some minutes Gladys finally retorts, "You can't make gravy with just Oxo, you need the juices of the meat and some pepper and salt."

Nurse Topsy says, "What juices, from what meat?"

I reply, somewhat taken aback, "The juices from the meat you have just cooked for your meal."

"Oh!" says Nurse Topsy, "But I don't eat meat, I only eat chicken and that comes out of the freezer and into the microwave and I've never seen any juices."

I look at Gladys , Gladys looks at me, Nurse Topsy smiles and walks away and I proceed to the next patient.

I am approaching a bed in which a new patient is sitting up, propped with several pillows and the patient is resplendent in dazzling, embroidered nightwear and wearing spectacles which are 'out-of- this world' and having 'shocking pink' finger nails.

I smile and offer my usual salutation "Good morning! would you care for a cup of tea or coffee?"

You must now try to imagine the scene: this patient is around 75 years of age, perhaps more, I am 75 years of age, balding with a little white hair around the side and back of my head.

"Good morning, laddy, and what tea and coffee do you have for me?"

I am somewhat taken aback. I have been rejuvenated to a "laddy", I have a large tea pot full of '99' tea, a container of powdered coffee, and a container of sugar and a jug kettle full of hot water.

"I'm sorry, madam," I say, "just ordinary tea and coffee."

"Is that ground coffee in the jug?"

"No, madam, that is the hot water to make the coffee."

"You should know by now that you need boiling water to make ground coffee, unless you are offering me that powdered rubbish, if you are I don't want it, I'll have tea!"

Having now become a little frustrated, I commence to pour a cup of tea.

"Do you take sugar in your tea?" I ask.

"Sugar! Sugar! only lemon in Earl Grey, it is Earl Grey isn't it, not that awful hospital tea we have at breakfast?"

"No, madam, it is not Earl Grey and no, madam, it is not the tea you had for breakfast, I made this fresh pot of tea a few minutes ago but if it is not to your liking I will serve the other ladies, excuse me!"

I am now at the closed door of one of the side wards, where individual patients reside for various reasons. Bill is here, he has been quite a long stay patient, but is now well on the road to recovery and awaiting discharge to suitable sheltered accommodation. We have been on good terms for some months now and are quite good at giving each other a spot of back-chat. I knock on the door and step inside. Bill is in bed asleep (it is now almost 10.15 hours)

"C'mon, wakey wakey," I call, "outside on parade, jump to it!"

Bill opens his eyes and looks at me " Oh gawd! Not you today, why can't you let a fellow sleep?"

"C'mon," I repeat, "Coffee, two sugars and one digestive biscuit, do you want it or shall I pour it down the sink?"

He pulls up his sheet, covering his face, makes himself comfortable and replies from under the sheet, "Push off, you're worse than the nurses and they take some beating!" I leave his coffee and biscuit on his bedside table and move to the next ward. Bill will come along to the kitchen later in his wheelchair and return his dirty cup, accompanied by some such remark as "Thanks for the coffee, Mate, and thank Gawd you've got tomorrow off, maybe I can get a morning's sleep without you disturbing me."

Well, we have had a laugh at my expense, let's look at another side of hospital life; how about the nurses? Oh yes! no one is excluded from the rigours and laughter of life in a hospital ward, don't worry, the doctors' time will come later!"

I am about my duties as "Mr.Tea Man" and I enter annexe B; this is a section reserved for male patients. I bid them "Good morning, gentlemen" and commence my routine. A nurse enters the annexe with the usual happy and courteous salutation and proceeds to draw the curtains around Mr.Bloggs' bed.

"Come along, Mr.Bloggs, time to get dressed, you've had your bath, and we can't have you lying around on your bed all day!"

You must appreciate the curtains are drawn all round the bed and I can see nothing. "Now, Mr.Bloggs, or would you prefer me to call you Ted?"

"You can call me what you like, but get out and leave me alone, I'm not a child."

"Come now, Ted, you know you need some help, you almost had a nasty fall yesterday, didn't you? Now come along, there's a good fellow."

There is a long spell of shuffling and mumblings from Mr.Bloggs then "Socks, vest, pants, shirt, trousers, there we are, Ted! Socks first? Here we go, let's put your first sock on your bad leg, this is your bad leg, isn't it? Oh! the other leg is the bad one, right, here we go then."

There are groans of pain and ouches of protest from Ted. "There, Ted, that wasn't too bad, was it? Come along, now the other one. There that's fine, we are getting along fine, aren't we?"

"Why don't you push off and do something useful while I dress myself?" says Ted. "Fuss, fuss, fuss all the time, just leave me alone."

"Now, Ted, it's no good being cross with me, you know you can't manage on your own. Now then, off with those pyjamas, that's fine, now pants first O.K."

More grunts from Ted as nurse gets underway. "Left leg first, that's fine, now the other leg, there, that was not too bad, was it? Let's try the vest now. It's what, Ted? Oh! you think it's too hot for a vest, O.K. let's pop on your shirt next then. There we are, Ted, don't you look smart, nice clean shirt, you look a proper gentleman. You what, Ted? Oh! yes, I know gentlemen wear trousers, well sit yourself down and we will try the trousers next."

I have served my patients with their requirements of tea or coffee and I leave the annexe and the nurse and poor Mr.Bloggs in his partially dressed state.

I now enter the main ward reserved for the female patients. There are some very sick ladies here and I have come to be amazed at how some of these dear old ladies suffer the adversities of life with a smile, while there are others who make life difficult for themselves and the nursing staff.

To come to the point however, I am now in the ward and I am confronted by a record trolley, (Medical records, not pop music records), a consultant and his entourage of house officers. With some difficulty, I guide my tea trolley to the first bed, and the consultant says to his flock, "Yes, that is quite correct, now who's next? Ah! yes, Mrs.Fry."

From experience on the wards, I have come to learn that Mrs.Fry is 84 years young, is suffering the early stages of dementia, is recuperating from a nasty fall at her home, has no immediate family and takes three teaspoons full of sugar in her tea. The latter information is most important to me, but I do not think the consultant is at all concerned!

The medical team approach Mrs.Fry's Bed but do not pull the curtains. The consultant opens fire - "Hello, Mrs.Fry, and how are you this fine morning?"

Mrs.Fry informs the consultant she is quite well and would like to go home.

"Yes, we'll talk about that later, Mrs.Fry, first of all there are just a few questions I would like to ask you. Do you know what day it is today?"

"Yes, of course I do, it's Monday, my pension day and I want to go and collect it." (actually it's Friday)

"Do you know what month it is?"

Mrs.Fry hesitates and says, "Yes, of course, it's October." (actually it's May)

"And do you know what year we are in, Mrs.Fry?"

"1948, sir!"

"That's wonderful Mrs.Fry, you're doing very well, just a few more questions and I'll leave you to rest. Can you tell me where you are at the moment, Mrs.Fry?"

"In bed, sir."

Chorus of laughter from all the doctors.

"Yes that's very good, Mrs.Fry, quite correct, but can you tell me what this building is where you are in bed?"

"Ah!" says Mrs.Fry with a little hesitation, "Oh yes, I remember - Ward E!"

Consultant, "No you are a little confused, Mrs.Fry."

Mrs.Fry interrupts, "Ah yes, I remember now, no I was in Ward E, but those nice men with the stretcher thing moved me away and took me to Winton. Yes that's right, I'm in Winton Hospital now and I am going home tomorrow."

Poor, dear Mrs.Fry, at the time of writing this book she was still at Barry House, she was steadily becoming even more confused, she could only walk with the aid of a wheeled frame and found it very difficult to feed herself. Life can be so sad.

Being "The Tea Man" at Barry House is a rewarding, satisfying, interesting and at times a mind-boggling pastime. You have male patients, you have female patients, you have visitors who have long periods to wait before they see their loved ones and are most grateful for a relaxing cup of tea. You have pleasant patients and you have extremely rude patients, you have patients with whom you can strike up a friendly relationship and you have patients you hope will not be there next time you go on duty; life is full of surprises at Barry House.

There are 'nil' by mouth patients, there are diabetic patients with varying degrees of dementia, some not strong enough to hold and control a cup and saucer, so you have to supply their drink in a lip beaker. There are patients with restricted

PER ARDUA PRO PATRIA

fluid intakes and patients on semi-solids only, Oh! no serving tea at Barry House is not like serving tea at 'Joe's Cafe', it can be quite nerve racking.

Have I told you the story of Mr.Briggs? Mr.Briggs is not a violent man, a very angry man, but not violent. You will appreciate that I am a rather tall individual, and when a tall person looks down on to a low trolley, it is sometimes difficult to estimate whether a cup is full or not. On this particular occasion I asked Mr.Briggs if he would like his usual cup of tea and he replied "Why the ——hell shouldn't I?" I poured his tea, gave him a biscuit and left his bay to serve patients in the adjoining bay.

I had only served one gentleman in the adjoining bay when I heard such a commotion in Mr.Briggs' section. Commotions are not my problem, so I carried on with my duties, only to be interrupted by a rather flustered nurse pursuing me with a cup of tea in her hand.

"Mr.Briggs!"

"Yes," I said, "What about Mr.Briggs?"

"I'm sorry," apologised the nurse. "Mr.Briggs says if he can't have a full cup of tea, you know what you can do with your tea, half a —— cup and one biscuit, what about some decent service."

In view of Mr.Briggs' strong language and his rudeness to the nurse, I returned to his bay, filled his cup with cold water, took it to his table and having given him the very last biscuit in my tin, I retrieved this one and only biscuit, gave it to another patient and went on my way. I don't think Mr.Briggs appreciated my actions, he hasn't spoken to me since! Except to say a very curt "Yes" when I ask him "Would you care for a cup of tea?"

Of course, another very interesting feature in the life of "The Tea Man" are the requests received from some of the patients, for example:-

"Only half a cup please,"

"No sugar, thank you,"

"Four large spoons of sugar, please,"

"I would like a very weak tea please, half tea, the rest milk and water , no sugar,"

"Tea with no sugar or milk,"

"Can I have a black coffee please , with sugar and milk," (Yes! that puzzled me too) "May I have a cup of hot milk please,"

"Young man, do you have any hot water? You do? Oh good, I'll just have a cup of hot water, thank you."

As I told you earlier it's not like 'Joe's Cafe' in this job.

PER ARDUA PRO PATRIA

Then of course we have the little incidentals. These are the little tasks I am asked to perform by and for the patients.

"Excuse me, young man" (I'm still 75 years of age although at times I feel almost 100) "Young man, would you pass me my handbag?"

"Certainly, madam, where is it?"

"I'm not quite certain, it could be in my locker, it could be under my bed, or I may have left it in the toilet."

After almost ten minutes of searching by a physiotherapist and myself, the lady in question retorts, "Oh! silly me, I'm sitting on it!"

"Excuse me, sir, I am unable to bend forward, would you be kind enough to put my slippers on for me?"

"Hey, guv, 'and us me fawc teef, oi can't reach 'em from 'ere."

"Young man,"

"I'm 75 years of age and... oh! never mind!"

"Young man, would you be so kind as to obtain for me an additional pillow, I'm not at all comfortable."

"By the way, will you boil me a mug of milk when you return to the kitchen."

DENNIS WILTSHIRE

"Would you be so kind as to pass me my walking frame please, I would get it myself only I can't walk without it."

"Would you please fetch me a commode immediately? I've been waiting for ages."

I explain that I am not permitted to execute nurse duties, but that I will find a nurse to help; I return with a nurse to be greeted with the words, "Don't bother, it's too late now anyway."

"Excuse me, sir, could I have a word with you? I just wanted to say that I have been in Barry House now for 12 weeks, and I would like to take this opportunity to thank you and all the ladies of The League who so kindly give up your time to bring us our tea and coffee."

Such remarks do boost our morale. I must introduce this lady to Mr. Briggs!

"Do you have such a thing as an aspirin? I've got a terrible headache."

"I'm sorry," I remark, "I am unable to hand out any medication. I'll fetch a nurse for you."

"Oh no! don't bother, they will not give me one, I've already asked!"

"Thank you for my coffee, would you be so kind as to lift me up so that I can drink it?"

PER ARDUA PRO PATRIA

"I'm sorry, but I'm not permitted to handle patients. I'll call a nurse for you."

"Oh no, don't bother, dear, I've been pressing my attention button for some minutes now, I think the nurses are much too busy elsewhere."

"Is that an RAF tie you are sporting, old chap?"

"Yes, sir."

"Good show, nice to meet you fellows, grand job you did for us, grand job. I say, you fellows, this chappie is an ex RAF type. Good show, Very typical, what?"

I am now confronted by an elderly gentleman who, for the past few weeks just looks at me when I pass his bed. He never has tea or coffee, he never has a biscuit, he never speaks to me, I do not speak to him anymore, for I know I shall receive no reply. He just looks at me without any sign of recognition. He seems a gentle man, a quiet man, I will not even give this man a name. And I think as I pass him by, "There, but for the Grace of God..."

To complete this little book, I would like to take this opportunity to say to all my contemporaneous colleagues who are active members of The League: "Thank you for the time and effort you afford patients and staff at the hospital."

To those who are not active members may I say: "Come and join us in our efforts to help those really in need, we need your help."

To those who have been active for so many years and have been overtaken by limits of age, ill health and other infirmities: "Thank you, God Bless you and rest your weary bodies in peace and contentment."

Finally, to the nursing staff of Barry House, may I say: "Thank you for all your help and encouragement."

I remain,

Yours sincerely,

"The Tea Man of Barry House."